NURSERY RHYMES

Mother Goose

MOTHER GOOSE RHYMES

Sleepytime

BEDTIME NURSERY RHYMES

compiled by Terry Pierce ∾ illustrated by Barbara Vagnozzi

PICTURE WINDOW BOOKS
Minneapolis, Minnesota

Special thanks to our advisers for their expertise:

Terry Flaherty, Ph.D., Professor of English
Minnesota State University, Mankato

Susan Kesselring, M.A., Literacy Educator
Rosemount–Apple Valley–Eagan (Minnesota) School District

Editors: Christianne Jones and Dodie Marie Miller
Designer: Tracy Davies
Page Production: Angela Kilmer
Art Director: Nathan Gassman
The illustrations in this book were created digitally.

Editor's Note: Editorial and formatting decisions for most
of the nursery rhymes in this book were based on the
following source: *The Random House Book of Mother
Goose* (1986), selected and illustrated by Arnold Lobel.

Picture Window Books
5115 Excelsior Boulevard
Suite 232
Minneapolis, MN 55416
877-845-8392
www.picturewindowbooks.com

Library of Congress Cataloging-in-Publication Data
Pierce, Terry.
Sleepytime : bedtime nursery rhymes / compiled by Terry
Pierce ; illustrated by Barbara Vagnozzi.
p. cm. – (Mother Goose rhymes)
Summary: An illustrated collection of twenty nursery
rhymes about bedtime.
ISBN-13: 978-1-4048-2345-7 (library binding)
ISBN-10: 1-4048-2345-X (library binding)
ISBN-13: 978-1-4048-2351-8 (paperback)
ISBN-10: 1-4048-2351-4 (paperback)
1. Nursery rhymes. 2. Bedtime–Juvenile poetry.
3. Children's poetry. [1. Nursery rhymes. 2. Bedtime–
Poetry.] I. Beer, Barbara Vagnozzi, ill. II. Mother Goose.
Selections. III. Title. IV. Title: Bedtime nursery rhymes.
PZ8.3.P558643Sle 2006
398.3–dc22 [E]   2006027247

TABLE OF CONTENTS

MOTHER
GOO

SE

NURSERY RHYMES ABOUT BEDTIME

BEDTIME is a SPECIAL TIME. The MOON and STARS come out. ANIMALS, CHILDREN, and GROWN-UPS all get ready for sleep. Snuggle down, listen to these bedtime rhymes, and hear the sounds of sweet slumber. Are you ready to drift into dreamland?

THE MAN IN THE MOON

The Man in the Moon
  looked out of the moon,
Looked out of the moon and said,
"'Tis time for all children on the earth
To think about getting to bed!"

DIDDLE, DIDDLE, DUMPLING

Diddle, diddle, dumpling, my son John,
Went to bed with his trousers on;
One shoe off, and one shoe on,
Diddle, diddle, dumpling, my son John.

EARLY TO BED

The cock crows in the morn
To tell us to rise,
And he that lies late
Will never be wise:

For early to bed
And early to rise
Is the way to be healthy
And wealthy and wise.

LITTLE BOY BLUE

Little Boy Blue, come blow your horn,

The cow's in the meadow, the sheep's in the corn.

But where is the little boy tending the sheep?

He's under the haystack fast asleep.

Will you wake him? No, not I,

For if I do, he's sure to cry.

TWINKLE, TWINKLE, LITTLE STAR

Twinkle, twinkle, little star,
How I wonder what you are!
Up above the world so high,
Like a diamond in the sky.
Twinkle, twinkle, little star,
How I wonder what you are!

When the blazing sun is gone,
When he nothing shines upon,
Then you show your little light,
Twinkle, twinkle, all the night.
Twinkle, twinkle, little star,
How I wonder what you are!

Then the traveler in the dark
Thanks you for your tiny spark;
He could not see which way to go,
If you did not twinkle so.
Twinkle, twinkle, little star,
How I wonder what you are!

GOOD NIGHT, SLEEP TIGHT

Good night, sleep tight,
Don't let the bedbugs bite.

I SEE THE MOON

I see the moon,
And the moon sees me,
And the moon sees somebody
I want to see.
God bless the moon,
And God bless me,
And God bless the somebody
I want to see.

13

SLEEP, BABY, SLEEP

Sleep, baby, sleep,
Thy father guards the sheep;
Thy mother shakes the dreamland tree
And from it fall sweet dreams for thee,
Sleep, baby, sleep.

Sleep, baby, sleep,
Our cottage vale is deep:
The little lamb is on the green,
With woolly fleece so soft and clean—
Sleep, baby, sleep.

Sleep, baby, sleep,
Down where the woodbines creep;
Be always like the lamb so mild,
A kind and sweet and gentle child,
Sleep, baby, sleep.

STAR LIGHT

Star light, star bright,
First star I see tonight,
I wish I may, I wish I might,
Have the wish I wish tonight.

⌒ ROCK-A-BYE, BABY ⌒

Rock-a-bye, baby, on the tree top,

When the wind blows the cradle will rock;

When the bough breaks the cradle will fall,

Down will come baby, cradle, and all.

GOOD NIGHT

Little baby, lay your head
On your pretty cradle-bed;
Shut your eye-peeps, now the day

And the lights are gone away;
All the clothes are tucked in tight;
Little baby dear, good night.

18

ON SATURDAY NIGHT I LOST MY WIFE

On Saturday night I lost my wife,
And where do you think I found her?
Up in the moon, singing a tune,
And all the stars around her.

COME OUT TO PLAY

Boys and girls, come out to play,
The moon doth shine as bright as day;
Leave your supper and leave your sleep,
And meet your playfellows in the street;

Come with a whoop and come with a call,
Come with a good will, or not at all.
Up the ladder and down the wall,
A halfpenny roll will serve us all.
You find milk and I'll find flour,
And we'll have a pudding in half an hour.

TO BED

Come, let's to bed,
Says Sleepy-head;
Sit up awhile, says Slow;
Hang on the pot,
Says Greedy-gut,
We'll sup before we go.

To bed, to bed,
Cried Sleepy-head,
But all the rest said No!
It is morning now;
You must milk the cow,
And tomorrow to bed we go.

GO TO BED LATE

Go to bed late,
Stay very small;
Go to bed early,
Grow very tall.

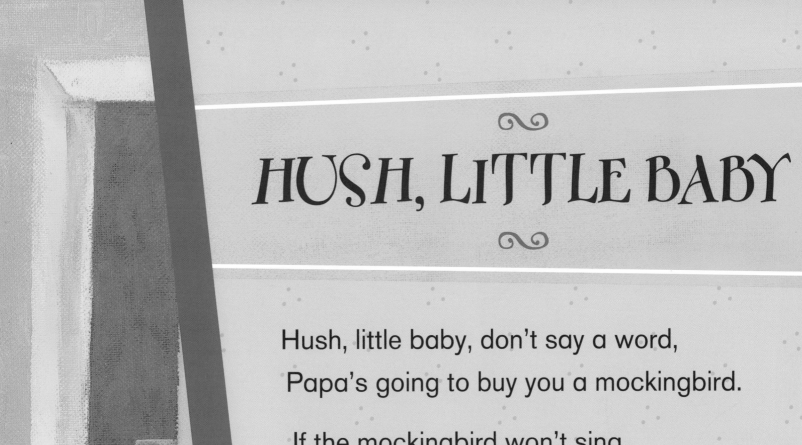

HUSH, LITTLE BABY

Hush, little baby, don't say a word,
Papa's going to buy you a mockingbird.

If the mockingbird won't sing,
Papa's going to buy you a diamond ring.

If the diamond ring turns to brass,
Papa's going to buy you a looking glass.

If the looking glass gets broke,
Papa's going to buy you a billy goat.

If the billy goat runs away,
Papa's going to buy you another today.

ROCK-A-BYE, BABY

Rock-a-bye, baby,
Thy cradle is green;
Father's a nobleman,
Mother's a queen;

And Betty's a lady,
And wears a gold ring,
And Johnny's a drummer,
And drums for the king.

HUSH-A-BYE

Hush-a-bye, baby,
Daddy is near,
Mamma is a lady,
And that's very clear.

~ GO TO BED FIRST ~

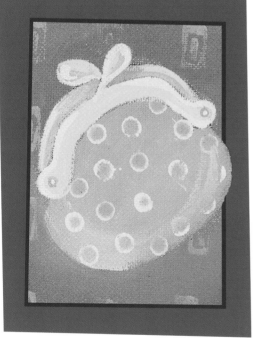

Go to bed first,
A golden purse;

Go to bed second,
A golden pheasant;

Go to bed third,
A golden bird.

WEE WILLIE WINKIE

Wee Willie Winkie runs through the town,

Upstairs and downstairs in his nightgown;

Rapping at the window, crying through the lock,

Are the children all in bed, for now it's eight o'clock?

29

THE HISTORY OF NURSERY RHYMES AND
MOTHER GOOSE

Nursery rhymes circulated orally for hundreds of years. In the 18th century, collectors wrote down the rhymes, printed them, and sold them to parents and other adults to help them remember the rhymes so they could share them with children.

Some of these collections were called "Mother Goose" collections. Nobody knows exactly who Mother Goose was (though there are plenty of myths about her), but she was probably a respected storyteller. Occasionally the rhymes commented on real people and events. The meaning of many of the rhymes has been lost, but the catchy rhythms remain.

Mother Goose nursery rhymes have evolved from many sources through time. From the 1600s until now, the appealing rhythms, rhymes, humor, and playfulness found in these verses, stories, and concepts contribute to what readers now know as Mother Goose nursery rhymes.

TO LEARN MORE

AT THE LIBRARY

Parmenter, Wayne. *Mother Goose Bedtime Rhymes.* Lincolnwood, Ill.: Publications International, 2002.

Rescek, Sanja. *Twinkle, Twinkle, Little Star and Other Bedtime Nursery Rhymes.* Wilton, Conn.: Tiger Tales, 2006.

Sattgast, L. J. *The Nursery Bedtime Book.* Sistes, Ore.: Gold 'n' Honey Books, 1995.

ON THE WEB

FactHound offers a safe, fun way to find Web sites related to this book. All of the sites on FactHound have been researched by our staff.

1. Visit *www.facthound.com*
2. Type in this special code: 140482345X
3. Click on the FETCH IT button.

Your trusty FactHound will fetch the best sites for you!

INDEX OF FIRST LINES

LOOK FOR ALL OF THE BOOKS IN THE MOTHER GOOSE RHYMES SERIES:

Counting Your Way: Number Nursery Rhymes

Cuddly Critters: Animal Nursery Rhymes

Forecasting Fun: Weather Nursery Rhymes

Friendly Faces: People Nursery Rhymes

Sleepytime: Bedtime Nursery Rhymes

Ticktock: Time Nursery Rhymes

Mother Goose

NURSERY RHYMES